P9-CSW-474

# COLONEL HARLAND SANDERS:
## KFC Creator

Sheila Griffin Llanas

Checkerboard
Library

An Imprint of Abdo Publishing
www.abdopublishing.com

www.abdopublishing.com

Published by Abdo Publishing, a division of ABDO, PO Box 398166, Minneapolis, Minnesota 55439. Copyright © 2015 by Abdo Consulting Group, Inc. International copyrights reserved in all countries. No part of this book may be reproduced in any form without written permission from the publisher. Checkerboard Library™ is a trademark and logo of Abdo Publishing.

Printed in the United States of America, North Mankato, Minnesota.
052014
092014

THIS BOOK CONTAINS
RECYCLED MATERIALS

Cover Photos: AP Images, Getty Images
Interior Photos: Alamy pp. 13, 27; AP Images pp. 1, 7, 15, 16, 22, 23; Corbis pp. 9, 14, 25;
    Getty Images pp. 5, 17, 19; iStockphoto p. 20; Library of Congress p. 21; Superstock p. 26;
    Wikimedia Commons p. 11

Series Coordinator: Megan M. Gunderson
Editors: Tamara L. Britton, Bridget O'Brien
Art Direction: Neil Klinepier

**Library of Congress Cataloging-in-Publication Data**

Llanas, Sheila Griffin, 1958- author.
  Colonel Harland Sanders : KFC creator / Sheila Griffin Llanas.
    pages cm. -- (Food dudes)
  Audience: Ages 9-12.
  ISBN 978-1-62403-318-6
1.  Sanders, Harland, 1890-1980--Juvenile literature. 2.  Kentucky Fried Chicken (Firm)--History--Juvenile literature. 3.  Restaurateurs--United States--Biography--Juvenile literature. 4. Businessmen--United States--Biography--Juvenile literature.  I. Title.
  TX910.5.S25L53 2015
  647.95092--dc23
  [B]
                            2014001420

# Contents

# Harland Sanders

What is better than a home-cooked meal? Home-cooked food you don't have to make yourself! That is what Colonel Harland Sanders began providing to customers at his gas station. As a side job, he made fried chicken hot, fresh, and fast. Over time, with a single recipe, the Colonel built Kentucky Fried Chicken. The iconic company is the most popular chicken restaurant chain in the world.

Harland David Sanders was born on a farm near Henryville, Indiana, on September 9, 1890. He had two younger **siblings**, Clarence and Catherine. Their parents, Wilbert and Margaret Ann Sanders, were farmers. They worked hard and earned little.

Harland's parents were resourceful. They survived the 1893 financial **depression**. And when Wilbert was injured doing farmwork, he opened a meat shop in Henryville. But when Wilbert died in 1896, the family struggled. Harland had to learn about hard work from a very early age.

Colonel Harland Sanders served hardworking families and travelers. For a time, his gas station became a success. But his chicken made him famous!

# Young Worker

To support three children, Harland's mother sewed clothing and cleaned homes. Yet not enough people needed her work. So, she got a job in a tomato-canning factory. Her hours were long. Sometimes, she stayed overnight with her brother near the factory. She left Harland at home to feed and care for his **siblings**. By age six, Harland was cooking meals.

As years passed, the family needed more income. When Harland turned ten, his mother sent him to work on their neighbor Charlie Norris's farm. The job paid two dollars a month plus meals. The farmer told Harland to go out to a field and clear brush. Harland was still a young boy. He got distracted by nature. All alone, he sat and watched squirrels and birds.

The farmer fired Harland for **loafing**. It was the first of many jobs Harland would lose or quit. Yet he felt terrible. He hated disappointing his mother. Harland devoted his life to making it up to her.

The area Harland grew up in is in Clark County in southeastern Indiana.

# Riding the Rails

Harland's next farm job was for Mr. Henry Monk. It paid four dollars a month plus meals. This time, Harland worked beside seasoned farmhands. At just 11 years old, he did the work of a grown man. He guided a team of horses and plowed fields. He fed and milked cows.

The work was hard, but home life was harder. Harland's mother remarried and the family moved. When an argument with his stepfather turned violent, Harland left home. He returned to Henryville. Now he was on his own.

Beginning at age 12, Harland worked as a farmhand for Sam Wilson. After two years, his uncle got him his first job outside of farmwork. He collected fares on a **streetcar**. Harland loved talking to the riders. And, the job inspired him to seek new opportunities.

Harland's size made him appear older than he was. So in 1906, he lied about his age. He said he was 21 instead of 16. Eager for adventure, Harland joined the US Army in October. On a ship to Cuba, he tended a herd of mules. It was a lot like farmwork. For most of the trip, Harland was seasick! His army tour lasted just four months.

Harland did not attend school past sixth grade.

Beginning in 1907, Harland worked railroad jobs. He assisted a blacksmith, shoveled sand, emptied ash buckets, and pounded stakes. Finally, he got a chance to work on trains instead of just around them. With his big size, Harland landed the tough job of feeding the engine with coal by hand. As he rode the rails, Harland saw the state of Alabama.

# A Service Station

One night in 1909, Sanders's train made its stop in Jasper, Alabama. Outside a movie theater, he met Josephine "Josie" King. The two dated for a few weeks and then married. The couple went on to have three children, Margaret, Harland Jr., and Mildred.

Sanders now had a family of his own to support. Railroad work took Sanders far from home. This was hard on his family. It was time to find a new way to earn a living.

Searching for jobs, Sanders **hitchhiked**. One day, he got a ride with a general manager of Standard Oil Company of Kentucky. He told Sanders about a **service station** in Nicholasville, Kentucky, that was in need of a good operator. He asked if Sanders wanted the job. Sanders said yes!

Sanders liked being his own boss, and he liked serving people. He filled cars with gasoline. Then, he took extra steps. He washed windows and **inflated** tires for no charge. He kept the station open early and late. With such excellent service, Sanders operated the best service station around. He sold more gas than any other station in the area.

Like many others, Sanders could not survive the stock market crash in 1929 and a drought that followed. Almost every business suffered at the start of the **Great Depression**. Sanders had to close his gas station. He was not out of work for long, though. His hard work had impressed people at Shell Oil Company in Middlesboro, Kentucky.

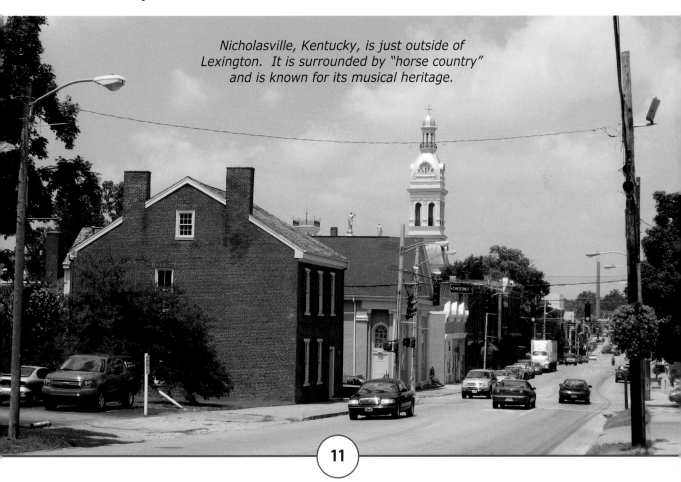

*Nicholasville, Kentucky, is just outside of Lexington. It is surrounded by "horse country" and is known for its musical heritage.*

# Sanders Cafe

Shell Oil gave Sanders a new station to run in 1930. This one was in Corbin, which was in a coal-mining area of eastern Kentucky. The station sat beside Highway 25. It was an easy stop for travelers.

Sanders ran the new gas station as well as the first. He always looked for extra services to provide. Many people wanted directions to nearby restaurants. But Sanders was a good cook. So instead of sending hungry people away, he began offering hot meals. He cleaned out an extra storage room and set the family dining table in there.

Sanders knew little about restaurants. He did not offer menus. Six guests at a time shared one table. Truck drivers and businessmen sat next to tourists. They ate whatever food Sanders cooked that day. Soon, strangers ate dinner at his family's table on a regular basis. When there were a lot of customers, Sanders fed the guests first. His family waited until he cooked more food.

Sanders served hot ham or fried chicken with cooked greens and hot biscuits. It was not fancy restaurant food. It was good, hearty Southern food, of the kind local farm families ate. Sanders had grown up eating this food. He had been cooking it since he was a young boy.

Over time, Sanders Service Station became Sanders Service Station and Cafe. When the restaurant took off, it became Sanders Cafe and Service Station. Once a hotel was added, it was called Sanders Court and Cafe.

SANDERS CAFE

KFC

drive thru

7PC VALUE MEAL $9.99

COMMONWEALTH OF KENTUCKY

BIRTHPLACE OF
KENTUCKY FRIED CHICKEN

In 1932 Colonel Harland Sanders bought the small restaurant near this site. Here he combined good cooking, hard work and showmanship to build regional fame for his fine food. His restaurant and a motel, now gone, flourished. To serve his patrons better Sanders constantly experimented with new recipes and cooking methods. Here he created, developed and perfected his world famous Kentucky Fried Chicken recipe. In 1956 plans were announced for a Federal highway to by-pass Corbin. Threatened with the traffic loss, Sanders, then 66 - and undaunted, sold the restaurant and started travelling 'America selling' seasoning, and his recipe for fried chicken to 'other restaurants. His success in this effort began the world's largest commercial food service system and made Kentucky a household word around 'the world.
Presented by the innumerable friends of Kentucky's greatest goodwill ambassador

THIS IS A SMOKE FREE FACILITY

# The Colonel

In 1949, Colonel Sanders wore a black suit and tie. His famous white suit and black tie came later!

Selling hot meals started as a side business. Yet soon, it helped Sanders sell more gas. The family saw success, but then it suffered a personal sadness. After minor surgery in 1932, Sanders's son, Harland Jr., got an infection and died. He was just 20 years old.

As years passed, Sanders needed more space to feed all of his customers. So, he opened a new restaurant. It could seat 142 people. In 1937, he also added a motel. Sanders had very high standards. He was devoted to service, quality, and improvement.

Sanders's restaurant was a source of Kentucky pride. In 1936, Governor Ruby Laffoon praised Sanders's contribution to the state's cuisine. He named him to the Honorable Order of Kentucky Colonels. Lieutenant Governor Lawrence Weatherby also named Sanders a colonel in 1949. From then on, he dressed like a Southern gentleman and went by Colonel Sanders.

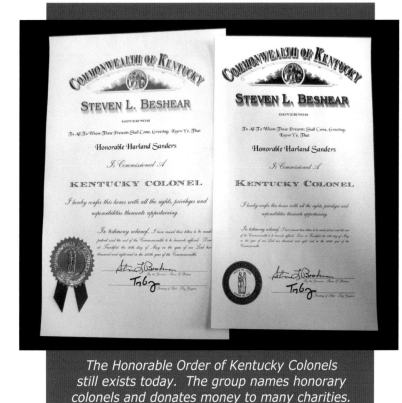

The Honorable Order of Kentucky Colonels still exists today. The group names honorary colonels and donates money to many charities.

In 1939, a fire destroyed Sanders Court and Cafe. The disaster did not stop Sanders. He rebuilt a bigger and better restaurant and motel. More and more, families stopped to buy hot, complete meals. Sanders called his food "home meal replacement." He described his chicken as "Sunday Dinner, Seven Days a Week."

# The Secret 11

*The Colonel's recipe is still kept secret today! Two companies each mix part of the recipe so no company has the full ingredient list.*

For years, Sanders experimented with his special recipe for fried chicken. In 1939, he perfected it. He **dredged** the meat in flour mixed with 11 herbs and spices. He loved the final flavor, and he kept the recipe secret.

Around the same time, Sanders perfected his cooking method. Frying on the stove took too long. Deep frying lowered

*Harman is credited with coming up with the slogan "finger lickin' good."*

quality. In 1939, Colonel Sanders bought a **pressure cooker**. Used with water, the new invention steamed vegetables. But Sanders used oil and made a pressure fryer. He experimented a lot. The result was tender, juicy chicken in just a few minutes.

Once again, as business went well, Sanders's personal life suffered. After 39 years together, he and Josephine divorced in 1947. Two years later, Sanders married Claudia Ledington Price, a waitress at his cafe. They remained together for the rest of his life.

Meanwhile, Sanders continued to learn about the restaurant industry. In 1950, he attended a National Restaurant Association convention in Chicago, Illinois. There, he met restaurant owner Pete Harman of Utah.

A year later, Sanders visited Harman in Salt Lake City. In Harman's restaurant kitchen, Sanders **dredged** chicken in his seasoned flour. He cooked it in a pressure cooker. He served his fried chicken, mashed potatoes, and gravy to Harman and his family. Harman didn't show it at first, but the meal was a hit!

# Life's Detour

Harman knew a good thing when he tasted it. He added "Colonel Sanders' Kentucky Fried Chicken" to the menu in his own restaurants. He posted a big picture of Colonel Sanders and advertised on the radio. It was great food with good advertising. Harman became the first Kentucky Fried Chicken **franchisee** in 1952. He paid Sanders five cents for every chicken he sold.

Sanders returned to running Sanders Court and Cafe. But in 1955, Highway 25 was rerouted. The new road **bypassed** Corbin! Cars no longer drove anywhere near Sanders's restaurant. Business died.

Sanders sold his property to pay his taxes and any remaining bills. After a lifetime of hard work, Sanders was nearly broke. He had a little money in savings and received only $105 a month from **Social Security**.

However, Sanders owned one thing of value. He knew how to make the best fried chicken! Making a brave choice, he decided to let more restaurants sell chicken using his original recipe. He needed to expand his chicken franchise operation. It certainly was not a side business anymore!

In 1957, Harman began selling Kentucky Fried Chicken in buckets. Customers could get 14 pieces of chicken, mashed potatoes, and gravy for $3.50.

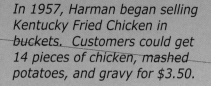

# Expanding

At first, Sanders and his wife did all the work themselves. Sanders mixed big tubs of his special blend of herbs and spices. He bought a lot of **pressure cookers**. He loaded the trunk of his car with these supplies. Then, he drove around to enlist new **franchisees**. He even slept in the car to save money! Claudia stayed home to fill the orders he called in.

In restaurants, Sanders fried samples of his recipe. He faced rejection many times, but he had always been a good salesman.

If restaurants agreed to sell his chicken, Sanders made "handshake deals." Like Harman, owners promised to pay a nickel for every order of chicken they served.

Sanders was a perfectionist. His chicken had to be cooked

*Sanders's recipe was rejected over 1,000 times. Restaurant owners didn't like to be told their chicken should be better!*

exactly right. Some **franchise** owners failed to follow instructions. They lost the rights to cook his original recipe.

In July 1959, the Colonel and Claudia moved to Shelbyville, Kentucky. On his big property, he added office and warehouse space. The new home became the Kentucky Fried Chicken headquarters.

Sanders worked tirelessly for four years. By 1960, more than 200 restaurants were selling Kentucky Fried Chicken in the United States and Canada. That year, Sanders was **inducted** into the American Restaurant Hall of Fame.

This bucket-shaped restaurant was completed in 1989. By then, the bucket was an important symbol of KFC.

# A Tough Choice

Kentucky Fried Chicken continued to expand. By 1964, there were more than 600 locations in the United States and Canada. There was even one overseas in England. The company attracted a lawyer named John Y. Brown Jr. Brown and a group of investors offered to purchase the company.

Sanders had to make a tough decision. His chicken was his pride and joy. But, the company had grown too big for him to manage alone.

So in 1964, Sanders signed a yellow piece of scrap paper and sold his company to Brown for $2

*Born in 1933, Brown (left) went on to serve as governor of Kentucky from 1979 to 1983.*

*Dave Thomas managed four Kentucky Fried Chicken franchises in Columbus, Ohio. In 1968, he sold them back to the company and became a millionaire! He then went on to launch his own fast food chain, Wendy's.*

million. Sanders was promised $40,000 every year for the rest of his life. This was later raised to $75,000 a year. He also kept the **franchises** in Canada. Not bad for a guy who was broke less than a decade earlier!

# Commercial Star

Kentucky Fried Chicken headquarters moved to Louisville, Kentucky, in 1969. The bold red-and-white striped restaurants were easily recognized and everywhere! Brown grew the number of **franchises** to more than 3,500 locations. And, the company continued expanding overseas.

Brown helped turn Kentucky Fried Chicken into a worldwide success. In 1971, he sold his interest in the company for a huge profit. The Colonel's chicken had become a multimillion dollar food chain.

The Colonel's image also remained important to the company. In commercials, he wore his white suit and boasted about his Original Recipe Chicken. His white hair, dark-rimmed glasses, and black string tie added to his distinguished image. Sanders also appeared on talk shows and game shows. He became a major public figure.

Sanders stayed busy outside of Kentucky Fried Chicken, too. He and Claudia opened a new restaurant on their property. They called it the Colonel's Lady. Later, the name changed to the Claudia Sanders Dinner House. There, the Colonel offered his two specialties, Southern hospitality and family-style food.

Sanders received the Horatio Alger Award in 1965. This award honors people who have succeeded through honesty and hard work and care about giving back.

# Generous Legacy

Until he was nearly 90, Sanders visited Kentucky Fried Chicken restaurants all around the world. He traveled 250,000 miles a year! He had fulfilled his desire to give customers a "home meal replacement."

In June 1980, Sanders was diagnosed with **leukemia**. Then he contracted **pneumonia**. Colonel Harland Sanders died on December 16, 1980, at the age of 90. He is buried in Louisville, Kentucky. More than 1,200 people attended his memorial service. To further honor him, the mayor asked that flags fly at half-staff.

The Colonel left behind a generous legacy. The Kentucky Fried Chicken Foundation, Inc., was formed in 1998. It was inspired by the Colonel's belief in hard work and giving back. It funds disaster relief, **scholarships** for education, and other causes.

*A sculpture of Sanders, made by his daughter Margaret, honors his grave.*

*Yum! Brands owns KFC, Taco Bell, and Pizza Hut.*

Kentucky Fried Chicken continued to thrive in Sanders's absence. In 1986, it was acquired by PepsiCo, Inc. The company name was shortened to KFC in 1991. KFC Corporation is still headquartered in Louisville, Kentucky. But today, it belongs to Yum! Brands, Inc.

KFC has more than 17,000 restaurants in more than 115 countries and territories. Every day, 12 million customers around the world eat KFC. More than 1 billion chicken dinners are served every year. The Colonel's image is still featured on KFC packaging. And people can still carry home his Sunday dinner.

# Timeline

| 1890 | Harland David Sanders was born on September 9 near Henryville, Indiana. |
| 1907 | Harland began working railroad jobs. |
| 1909 | Sanders married Josephine "Josie" King. |
| 1930 | Sanders began working at his Corbin, Kentucky, service station. |
| 1936 | Sanders was named to the Honorable Order of Kentucky Colonels. |
| 1939 | Sanders perfected his secret recipe of 11 herbs and spices. |
| 1949 | Sanders married Claudia Ledington Price. |
| 1952 | Pete Harman became the first Kentucky Fried Chicken franchisee. |
| 1955 | Sanders sold the Sanders Court and Cafe. |
| 1964 | Sanders sold Kentucky Fried Chicken for $2 million. |
| 1980 | After a short illness, Colonel Sanders died on December 16. |

# International Tastes

Over the years, KFC has expanded into more than 115 countries. Since customer tastes differ around the globe, KFC has changed its menus to fit. Each country has its own special offerings to go along with the Colonel's special blend of herbs and spices.

Australia: chocolate and caramel mousse

China: rice porridge with pork

India: potato patty sandwich

Kuwait: profiteroles

Singapore: chicken and rice

Thailand: shrimp donut

United Kingdom: toffee sundae

# Glossary

**bypass** - to provide a way around something.

**depression** - a period of economic trouble when there is little buying or selling and many people are out of work.

**dredge** - to coat food by sprinkling it with flour or sugar.

**franchise** - the right granted to someone to sell a company's goods or services in a particular place. The business operating with this right is also known as a franchise. A franchisee is someone who operates a franchise.

**Great Depression** - the period from 1929 to 1942 of worldwide economic trouble. There was little buying or selling and many people could not find work.

**hitchhike** - to travel by getting free rides from drivers passing by.

**induct** - to admit as a member.

**inflate** - to expand by filling with air or a gas.

**leukemia** (loo-KEE-mee-uh) - a disease marked by an abnormal increase in white blood cells. Leukemia is a kind of cancer.

**loafing** - doing no work.

**pneumonia** (nuh-MOH-nyuh) - a disease that affects the lungs. It may cause fever, coughing, or difficulty breathing.

**pressure cooker** - an airtight pot for cooking foods using steam and pressure.

**scholarship** - money or aid given to help a student continue his or her studies.

**service station** - a place that offers gasoline and other services for automobiles.

**sibling** - a brother or a sister.

**Social Security** - a US government program that provides money to people such as those who are no longer working.

**streetcar** - a vehicle that travels on tracks on city streets.

# Websites

To learn more about Food Dudes, visit **booklinks.abdopublishing.com**. These links are routinely monitored and updated to provide the most current information available.

# Index